SUMMER MATH WORKBOOK

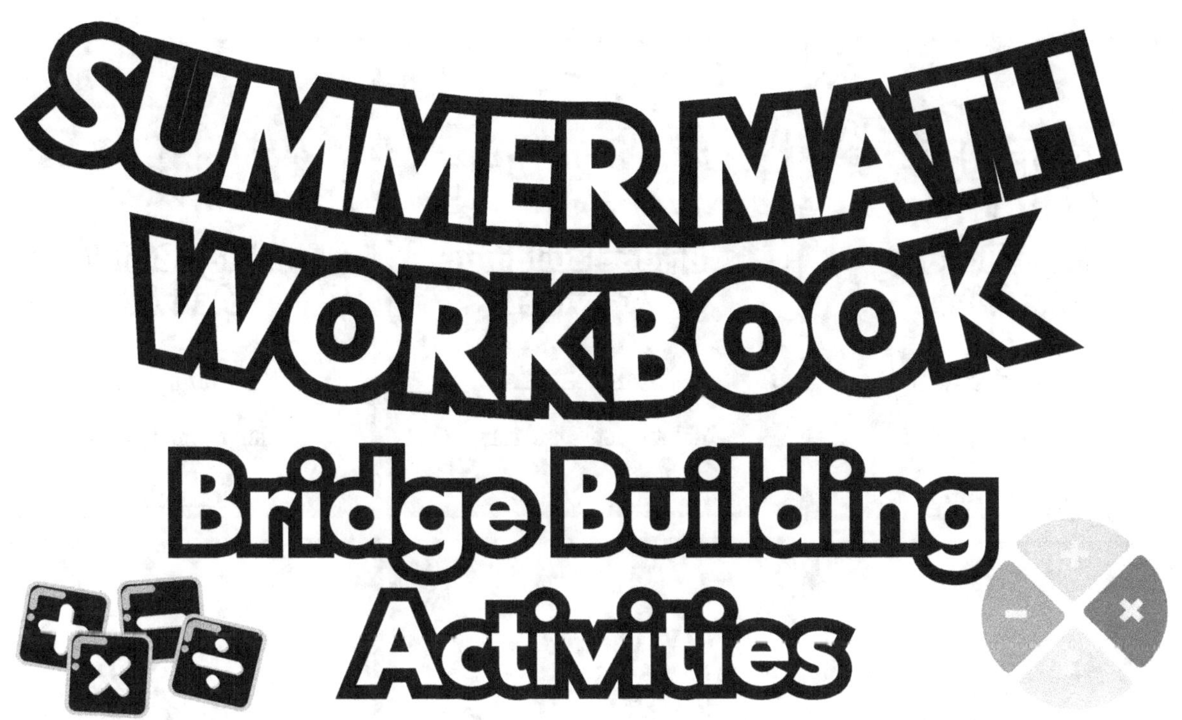

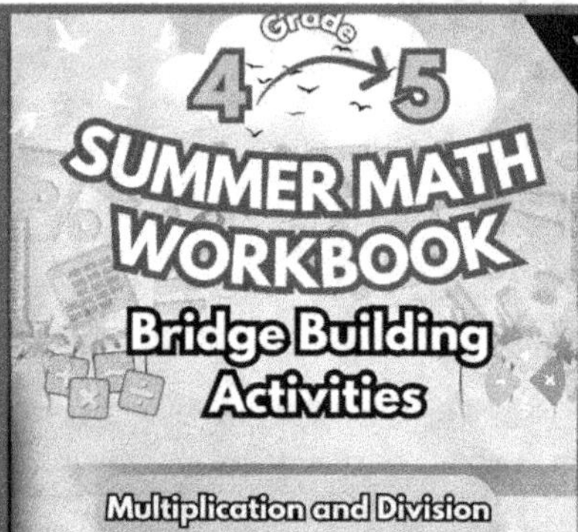

Grade 1 2
SUMMER MATH WORKBOOK
Bridge Building Activities
Number Sense
Addition and Subtraction
Place Value

Grade 2 3
SUMMER MATH WORKBOOK
Bridge Building Activities
Number Sense
Addition and Subtraction
Place Value

Grade 3 4
SUMMER MATH WORKBOOK
Bridge Building Activities
Number Sense
Addition and Subtraction
Place Value

Grade 4 5
SUMMER MATH WORKBOOK
Bridge Building Activities
Multiplication and Division
Place Value and Units
Fractions and Geometry

Grade 5 6
SUMMER MATH WORKBOOK
Bridge Building Activities
Multiplication and Division
Factors and Multiples
Fractions and Geometry

Grade 6 7
SUMMER MATH WORKBOOK
Bridge Building Activities
Arithmetic
Algebra
Geometry and Statistics

Grade 7 8
SUMMER MATH WORKBOOK
Bridge Building Activities
Ratio and Percentage
Algebra and Cartesian Plane
Geometry and Statistics

Grade 8 9
SUMMER MATH WORKBOOK
Bridge Building Activities
Ratio and Percentage
Algebra
Geometry and Graphing

Grade 9 10
SUMMER MATH WORKBOOK
Bridge Building Activities
Factoring and Distributing
Algebra
Geometry and Graphing

Introduction

As parents and educators, we understand the pivotal role that mathematics plays in shaping a child's academic journey and future success. Yet, the path to mathematical proficiency can often seem daunting, filled with challenges and complexities. That's where the transformative power of Summer Bridge Building Activities books comes into play, illuminating the way forward with clarity, precision, and purpose.

Summer vacation is a time for rest and relaxation, but it also presents the risk of the "summer slide," where students lose some of the academic gains they made during the school year. Summer Bridge Building Activities books are specifically designed to tackle this challenge, ensuring that your child stays academically engaged and prepared for the upcoming school year. These books provide a seamless bridge from one grade to the next, reinforcing essential skills and introducing new concepts that will give your child a head start.

Imagine your child eagerly diving into the pages of a Summer Bridge Building Activities book, greeted by clear, engaging content that demystifies complex mathematical concepts. With each turn of the pages, they embark on a journey of discovery, encountering thoughtfully curated practice questions that reinforce learning and sharpen problem-solving skills. As they unveil the answers to those questions, a sense of accomplishment blossoms within them — a tangible reward for their hard work and dedication.

Summer Bridge Building Activities books transcend traditional educational tools; they are meticulously crafted to build a deep and enduring understanding of mathematics. These books follow a sequential and logical progression, starting from fundamental principles and advancing to sophisticated problem-solving strategies. Each chapter is designed to build on the previous one, ensuring a solid and comprehensive foundation for future learning.

Parents, we yearn for nothing more than to see our children thrive academically and personally. We want to witness the spark of inspiration ignited within them as they overcome academic challenges with confidence and poise. Summer Bridge Building Activities books serve as indispensable partners in this noble endeavor, offering not just practice questions but the keys to unlocking a world of academic and personal opportunities.

Visualize the pride on your child's face as they master a challenging math concept, the joy they experience when their efforts yield results, and the confidence they gain with each success. These pages are designed to make learning math a positive, enriching, and deeply rewarding experience that will benefit them throughout their academic journey and beyond.

For educators, Summer Bridge Building Activities books are invaluable allies in the quest to cultivate mathematical proficiency in the classroom. Accompanied by comprehensive guides and readily available answers, instructors can focus on mentoring and nurturing their students, secure in the knowledge that these books provide a robust framework for effective learning.

Within the pages of Summer Bridge Building Activities books lies not just the promise of academic excellence, but the seeds of a brighter future. By integrating these resources into your child's summer routine, you are bestowing upon them the gifts of confidence, curiosity, and a lifelong love of learning.

Invest in your child's future today with Summer Bridge Building Activities books — because every great journey begins with a single step, and this step can change everything. Keep the momentum of learning alive over the summer, and watch your child soar to new academic heights.

Contents

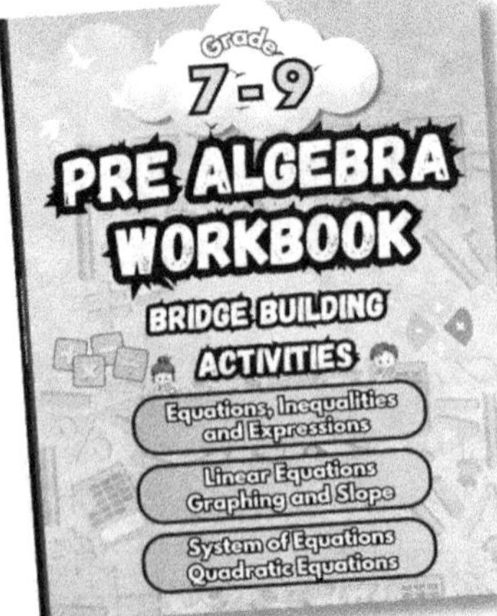

Grade 7 - 9
PRE ALGEBRA WORKBOOK
BRIDGE BUILDING ACTIVITIES
Equations, Inequalities and Expressions
Linear Equations Graphing and Slope
System of Equations Quadratic Equations

Grade 6 - 8
PRE ALGEBRA WORKBOOK
BRIDGE BUILDING ACTIVITIES
Equations One Side and Two Sides
Verbal Algebra Expressions
Linear Equations and Slope Order of Operations

Grade 5 - 6
PRE ALGEBRA WORKBOOK
BRIDGE BUILDING ACTIVITIES
Integers, Mixed Numbers Decimals and Fractions
Place Value Exponents and Roots
Percentage and Ratio Word Problems

PRE ALGEBRA WORKBOOK
for Beginners
Integers Fractions, Mixed Numbers
Place Value Exponents and Roots
Percentage Ratio Conversion

PRE ALGEBRA WORKBOOK
for Adults
Integers Percent and Ratio
Equations, Inequalities Expressions
Order of Operations

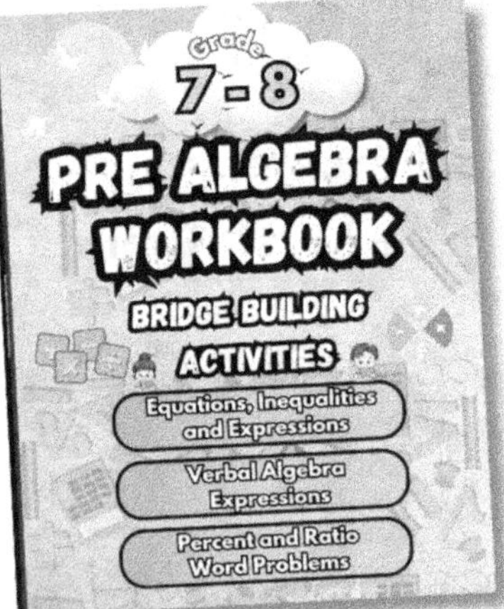

Grade 7 - 8
PRE ALGEBRA WORKBOOK
BRIDGE BUILDING ACTIVITIES
Equations, Inequalities and Expressions
Verbal Algebra Expressions
Percent and Ratio Word Problems

Grade 9 - 10
PRE ALGEBRA WORKBOOK
BRIDGE BUILDING ACTIVITIES
Equations and Inequalities Verbal Algebra
Linear and Quadratic Equations
System of Equations Polynomials

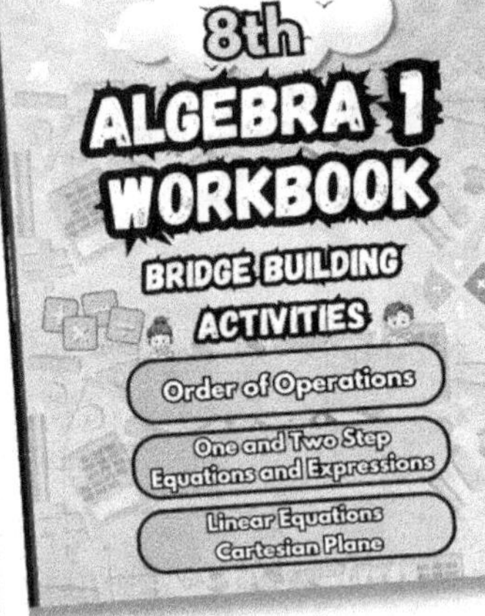

Grade 8th
ALGEBRA 1 WORKBOOK
BRIDGE BUILDING ACTIVITIES
Order of Operations
One and Two Step Equations and Expressions
Linear Equations Cartesian Plane

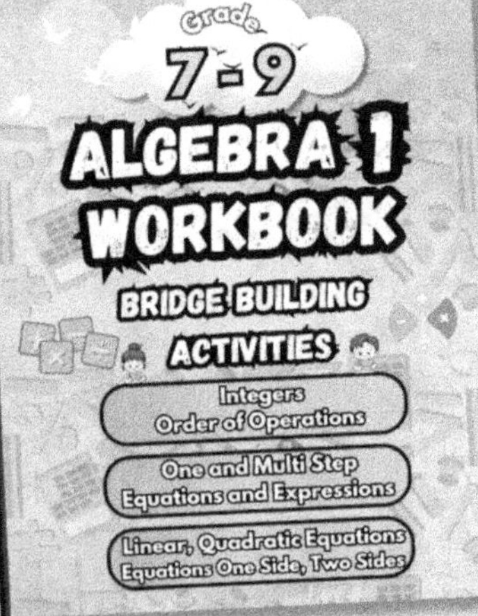

Grade 7 - 9
ALGEBRA 1 WORKBOOK
BRIDGE BUILDING ACTIVITIES
Integers Order of Operations
One and Multi Step Equations and Expressions
Linear, Quadratic Equations Equations One Side, Two Sides

Operations with Integers

Positive and negative integers are whole numbers that can represent quantities greater than zero and less than zero, respectively.

Positive Integers: Positive integers are whole numbers greater than zero. They are denoted by the numbers 1,2,3,4...

Negative Integers: Negative integers are whole numbers less than zero. They are denoted by placing a negative sign ("-") before the numbers, such as $-1,-2,-3,-4,...$

The positive integers are used to represent the number of objects, scores, etc. whereas the negative integers can be used to represent debt, losses, temperatures below freezing points, etc.

Let's solve some problems:

1. 6 – (– 8) – 9

- Start by simplifying within the parentheses:

  – (–8) becomes 8.

- Rewrite the expression with the simplified part:

  6 + 8 – 9.

- Now perform addition and subtraction from left to right:

  6 + 8 =1 4, then 14 – 9 = 5

2. (– 5) – (– 3) + 10

(–5) + 3 + 10

(–5) + 3 = – 2, then – 2 + 10 = 8

SUMMER ALGEBRA WORKBOOK

BUILDING ACTIVITIES

Operations with Integers

1. $4 - 10 + 4 =$

2. $(-3) + 3 + (-2) =$

3. $(-10) - (-4) =$

4. $4 + (-2) =$

5. $(-5) - 2 + (-2) =$

6. $3 - (-8) - 5 =$

7. $(-5) + (-2) + 1 =$

8. $2 - 2 + 4 =$

9. $10 + (-5) =$

10. $(-8) + (-2) - 8 =$

11. $(-6) + (-2) + (-3) =$

12. $(-2) + 10 + (-7) =$

13. $(-8) + (-9) - 4 =$

14. $(-8) + (-2) + (-6) =$

15. $(-8) - 8 + (-7) =$

16. $5 + (-7) - 1 =$

17. $(-3) + (-3) + (-8) =$

18. $(-5) + (-8) - 5 =$

19. $(-9) - 2 + (-9) =$

20. $9 + 1 - 10 =$

21. $9 - 6 + 1 =$

22. $5 + (-5) =$

23. $(-3) + 2 + (-10) =$

24. $(-5) - (-5) + 4 =$

25. $(-5) + 5 + (-7) =$

26. $4 - 7 - 4 =$

27. $4 - (-6) =$

28. $(-10) + 4 =$

29. $(-4) + (-5) + 10 =$

30. $10 - 1 - 5 =$

31. $(-8) - 3 =$

32. $(-9) + (-9) + (-10) =$

33. $9 - 4 + 10 =$

34. $6 - 5 + 4 =$

35. $3 - (-4) - 3 =$

36. $(-7) + (-7) - 8 =$

37. $(-9) - 4 + (-1) =$

38. $(-1) - (-2) + 3 =$

39. $9 - 5 + 3 =$

40. $1 + 7 - 5 =$

41. $(-1) + (-1) - 5 =$

42. $5 + (-8) + 5 =$

43. $7 - (-7) =$

44. $7 + 5 - 7 =$

45. $(-2) - (-8) + 8 =$

46. $2 - (-10) =$

47. $2 - 2 + 7 =$

48. $8 - (-8) - 8 =$

49. $1 + (-7) =$

50. $(-1) + 5 =$

51. $6 - (-1) =$

52. $10 + (-5) - 7 =$

53. $(-8) - 7 + (-5) =$

54. $(-6) + (-4) - 10 =$

55. $9 + 7 - 8 =$

56. $10 + (-1) + 2 =$

57. $5 + (-8) - 9 =$

58. $(-3) - (-5) + 1 =$

59. $9 - 4 + 1 =$

60. $(-4) + 9 =$

61. $8 - 4 + 1 =$

62. $(-9) + (-4) - 4 =$

63. $9 - (-6) - 7 =$

64. $(-3) - 8 + (-9) =$

65. $(-5) + (-4) + (-2) =$

66. $8 - 1 + 3 =$

67. $6 - 10 + 8 =$

68. $8 - 6 + 7 =$

Mixed Numbers and Improper Fractions

Mixed numbers and improper fractions are two different ways to represent the same value of a fraction.

1. **Mixed Number:** A mixed number is a combination of a whole number and a proper fraction. For example, $2\frac{1}{3}$ is a mixed number, where 2 is the whole number part and $\frac{1}{3}$ is the fraction part.

2. **Improper Fraction:** An improper fraction is a fraction where the numerator is greater than or equal to the denominator. For example, $\frac{7}{3}$ is an improper fraction because 6 is greater than 3.

To convert a mixed number to an improper fraction, you multiply the whole number by the denominator of the fraction, add the numerator, and then write the result over the original denominator. For example:

$$2\frac{1}{3} = \frac{2 \times 3 + 1}{3} = \frac{7}{3}$$

To convert an improper fraction to a mixed number, we divide the numerator by the denominator. The quotient becomes the whole number part, and the remainder becomes the numerator of the fraction. For example:

$$\frac{7}{3} = 2\frac{1}{3}$$

<u>Mixed Numbers: Addition and Subtraction</u>

To add or subtract mixed numbers, we follow similar steps as when adding or subtracting regular fractions. For instance:

Addition:

- <u>Add the whole numbers:</u> Add the whole number parts of the mixed numbers together.
- <u>Add the fractions:</u> Add the fractions parts of the mixed numbers together.
- <u>Simplify (if needed):</u> If the fraction part of the sum is an improper fraction, simplify it by converting it to a mixed number.

Subtraction:

- <u>Subtract the whole numbers:</u> Subtract the whole number part of the second mixed number from the whole number part of the first mixed number.
- <u>Subtract the fractions:</u> Subtract the fraction part of the second mixed number from the fraction part of the first mixed number.
- <u>Simplify (if needed):</u> If the fraction part of the difference is a negative fraction, borrow from the whole number part or simplify it by converting it to a mixed number.

Mixed Numbers: Multiplication and Division

To multiply or divide mixed numbers, we follow these steps:

Multiplication:

- Convert the mixed numbers to improper fractions: Multiply the whole number by the denominator of the fraction, then add the numerator. Write the result over the original denominator.
- Multiply the fractions: Multiply the numerators together to get the new numerator and multiply the denominators together to get the new denominator.
- Simplify (if needed): If the result is an improper fraction, simplify it by converting it back to a mixed number.

Division:

- Convert the mixed numbers to improper fractions:
- Invert the divisor: Flip the second fraction (the one you're dividing by) so that the division becomes multiplication.
- Multiply the fractions: Multiply the numerators together to get the new numerator and multiply the denominators together to get the new denominator.
- Simplify (if needed): If the result is an improper fraction, simplify it by converting it back to a mixed number.

Multiplication with whole numbers

To multiply a fraction by a whole number, we simply multiply the numerator of the fraction by the whole number while keeping the denominator the same.

For example, if we have $\frac{2}{3}$ and we want to multiply it by 5:

$$5 \times \frac{2}{3} = \frac{5 \times 2}{3} = \frac{10}{3}$$

Operations with Mixed Numbers

Calculate.

1. $8\frac{2}{6} + 2\frac{1}{3} =$ _______________________________

2. $1\frac{1}{5} + 2\frac{6}{10} =$ _______________________________

3. $4\frac{7}{9} \div 8\frac{1}{2} =$ _______________________________

4. $6\frac{2}{7} - 4\frac{7}{8} =$ _______________________________

5. $4\frac{2}{3} \div 4\frac{4}{6} =$ _______________________________

6. $9\frac{1}{5} - 8\frac{1}{4} =$ _______________________________

7. $8\frac{2}{5} - 7\frac{1}{6} =$ _______________________________

8. $9\frac{1}{2} \times 7\frac{9}{10} =$ _______________________________

9. $7\frac{4}{8} - 2\frac{2}{4} =$ _______________________________

10. $1\frac{4}{9} + 2\frac{4}{7} =$ _______________________________

11. $9\frac{1}{3} - 5\frac{8}{9} = $ _______________________

12. $8\frac{1}{6} + 3\frac{4}{8} = $ _______________________

13. $4\frac{4}{5} + 6\frac{2}{3} = $ _______________________

14. $7\frac{1}{2} \times 3\frac{8}{10} = $ _______________________

15. $4\frac{1}{4} + 1\frac{6}{7} = $ _______________________

16. $7\frac{2}{4} \times 8\frac{1}{8} =$ ___________

17. $2\frac{1}{5} \times 3\frac{2}{7} =$ ___________

18. $9\frac{1}{2} - 7\frac{2}{3} =$ ___________

19. $4\frac{2}{6} \times 8\frac{3}{9} =$ ___________

20. $8\frac{3}{10} + 8\frac{2}{8} =$ ___________

21. $5 \frac{3}{5} \div 6 \frac{2}{10} =$ ___________

22. $4 \frac{2}{3} \div 9 \frac{1}{2} =$ ___________

23. $8 \frac{2}{7} \times 7 \frac{1}{4} =$ ___________

24. $5 \frac{8}{9} - 1 \frac{4}{6} =$ ___________

25. $4 \frac{6}{8} + 4 \frac{4}{8} =$ ___________

26. $2\frac{3}{6} + 8\frac{4}{7} =$ _______________

27. $7\frac{2}{3} \div 4\frac{8}{10} =$ _______________

28. $9\frac{1}{2} - 8\frac{3}{5} =$ _______________

29. $8\frac{4}{9} \div 8\frac{1}{4} =$ _______________

30. $3\frac{4}{7} \times 4\frac{2}{9} =$ _______________

31. $7\frac{1}{3} + 4\frac{1}{6} =$ _______________

32. $6\frac{2}{4} \div 8\frac{9}{10} =$ _______________

33. $9\frac{7}{8} + 6\frac{1}{2} =$ _______________

34. $9\frac{1}{5} \div 7\frac{2}{3} =$ _______________

35. $9\frac{3}{7} - 1\frac{1}{10} =$ _______________

36. $4 \frac{4}{5} \div 7 \frac{1}{4} =$ _______________

37. $7 \frac{2}{8} \div 6 \frac{2}{9} =$ _______________

38. $8 \frac{3}{6} - 1 \frac{1}{2} =$ _______________

39. $7 \frac{6}{9} \times 6 \frac{4}{5} =$ _______________

40. $5 \frac{7}{8} \div 4 \frac{3}{4} =$ _______________

41. $8\frac{5}{7} \div 6\frac{4}{10} =$ _______________

42. $8\frac{3}{6} - 6\frac{1}{2} =$ _______________

43. $7\frac{2}{3} \times 8\frac{2}{6} =$ _______________

44. $6\frac{8}{10} - 1\frac{1}{4} =$ _______________

45. $5\frac{4}{8} \div 2\frac{4}{5} =$ _______________

<u>**Multiple Operations Fractions**</u>

Fraction multiple operations involve performing multiple arithmetic operations (addition, subtraction, multiplication, division) on fractions.

We follow (PEDMAS that stands for the order of operations in arithmetic) to solve multiple operations Fractions:

1. **Parentheses:** Perform operations inside parentheses first.

2. **Exponents:** Evaluate expressions with exponents or powers.

3. **Multiplication and Division:** Perform multiplication and division from left to right.

4. **Addition and Subtraction:** Perform addition and subtraction from left to right.

For example:

Let's solve the expression: $\frac{3}{4} + \frac{1}{2} \times \frac{2}{3}$

Step 1: Begin by performing the multiplication operation first:

$$= \frac{1 \times 2}{2 \times 4} = \frac{2}{6} = \frac{1}{3}$$

Step 2: Now rewrite the expression with the result of the multiplication:

$$\frac{3}{4} + \frac{1}{3}$$

Step 3: To add fractions, find a common denominator. In this case, the least common multiple (LCM) of 4 and 3 is 12.

Step 4: Rewrite both fractions with the common denominator:

$$\frac{9}{12} + \frac{4}{12}$$

Step 5: Add the numerators together and keep the common denominator:

$$\frac{13}{12} = 1\frac{1}{12}$$

Multiple Operations with Fractions

Find the solution.

1. $\left(\dfrac{1}{7} + \dfrac{1}{8}\right) \times \left(\dfrac{1}{9} + \dfrac{1}{5}\right) =$

2. $\dfrac{3}{10} + \dfrac{1}{10} + 2 =$

3. $\dfrac{1}{2} + \dfrac{1}{2} + 2 =$

4. $\dfrac{9}{10} \times \dfrac{6}{7} \times \dfrac{3}{4} =$

5. $\dfrac{5}{8} + \dfrac{5}{8} + 5 =$

6. $\left(\dfrac{1}{5} + \dfrac{8}{9}\right) \div \dfrac{3}{8} =$

7. $\left(\dfrac{5}{6} + \dfrac{3}{10}\right) \div \dfrac{8}{9} =$

8. $\dfrac{1}{6} \times \dfrac{1}{6} + \dfrac{1}{2} =$

9. $\left(\frac{1}{6} + \frac{1}{7}\right) - \left(\frac{5}{6} \times \frac{2}{9}\right) =$

10. $\frac{2}{3} + \frac{1}{10} + \frac{7}{8} + \frac{2}{7} =$

11. $\left(\frac{3}{5} \times \frac{5}{8}\right) + \left(\frac{2}{9} \times \frac{1}{3}\right) =$

12. $\frac{3}{8} \times \frac{3}{10} \times \frac{3}{10} =$

13. $\dfrac{3}{10} + \dfrac{1}{7} + \dfrac{4}{5} + \dfrac{1}{2} =$

14. $\left(\dfrac{5}{6} \times \dfrac{4}{5}\right) + \left(\dfrac{1}{6} \times \dfrac{1}{3}\right) =$

15. $\left(\dfrac{1}{4} \times \dfrac{7}{10}\right) + \left(\dfrac{2}{3} \times \dfrac{1}{3}\right) =$

16. $\dfrac{3}{4} + \dfrac{1}{7} + \dfrac{5}{8} + \dfrac{1}{7} =$

17. $\left(\dfrac{7}{9} \times \dfrac{1}{6}\right) + \left(\dfrac{5}{6} \times \dfrac{1}{3}\right) =$

18. $\left(\dfrac{1}{8} + \dfrac{3}{8}\right) - \left(\dfrac{1}{7} \times \dfrac{1}{8}\right) =$

19. $\dfrac{1}{5} + \dfrac{8}{9} + \dfrac{1}{6} =$

20. $\dfrac{1}{5} + \dfrac{2}{9} + 5 =$

21. $\dfrac{3}{10} + \dfrac{7}{9} + 6 =$

22. $\dfrac{8}{9} + \dfrac{4}{9} + 2 =$

23. $\left(\dfrac{1}{3} + \dfrac{1}{2}\right) \times \left(\dfrac{1}{4} + \dfrac{2}{9}\right) =$

24. $\left(\dfrac{1}{4} + \dfrac{1}{2}\right) \div \dfrac{1}{2} =$

25. $\dfrac{3}{8} \times \dfrac{3}{4} \times \dfrac{5}{8} =$

26. $\dfrac{1}{10} + \dfrac{2}{7} + \dfrac{8}{9} =$

27. $\dfrac{1}{4} \times \dfrac{1}{6} \times \dfrac{4}{7} =$

28. $\dfrac{4}{9} \times \dfrac{1}{2} + \dfrac{1}{4} =$

29. $\dfrac{2}{9} + \dfrac{8}{9} + 6 =$

30. $\left(\dfrac{1}{6} + \dfrac{7}{8}\right) \div \dfrac{3}{7} =$

31. $\dfrac{4}{5} + \dfrac{1}{6} - \dfrac{5}{8} =$

32. $\dfrac{3}{10} + \dfrac{1}{4} + \dfrac{5}{8} =$

33. $\left(\dfrac{9}{10} + \dfrac{1}{2}\right) \times \left(\dfrac{2}{3} + \dfrac{1}{10}\right) =$

34. $\dfrac{7}{10} + \dfrac{1}{2} + \dfrac{1}{6} =$

35. $\left(\dfrac{1}{10} + \dfrac{2}{5}\right) - \left(\dfrac{4}{7} \times \dfrac{7}{10}\right) =$

36. $\dfrac{1}{2} + \dfrac{2}{5} + \dfrac{9}{10} + \dfrac{3}{8} =$

37. $\dfrac{3}{10} + \dfrac{3}{4} - \dfrac{2}{9} =$

38. $\left(\dfrac{5}{8} + \dfrac{2}{5}\right) \times \left(\dfrac{4}{9} + \dfrac{3}{10}\right) =$

39. $\dfrac{1}{8} + \dfrac{2}{7} + \dfrac{1}{6} =$

40. $\left(\dfrac{3}{4} + \dfrac{5}{8}\right) \times \left(\dfrac{5}{6} + \dfrac{1}{4}\right) =$

Place Value and Expanded Notations

Place value tells us the value of a digit in a number based on where it's placed.

Imagine we have the number 2,735,987,647.52843. It has 15 digits.

Now, each digit holds a special place. Let's break down the number 2,735,987,647.52843:

- The digit 2 is in billions place. Its value is 2 × 1,000,000,000=2,000,000,000
- The digit 7 is in hundred millions place. Its value is 7 × 100,000,000=700,000,000
- The digit 3 is in the ten millions place. Its value is 3 × 1,000,000=30,000,000.
- The digit 5 is in the millions place. Its value is 5 × 1,000,000=5,000,000.
- The digit 9 is in the hundred thousands place. Its value is 9×100,000=900,000.
- The digit 8 is in the ten thousands place. Its value is 8×10,000=80,000.
- The digit 7 is in the thousands place. Its value is 7×1,000=7,000.
- The digit 6 is in the hundreds place. Its value is 6×100=600.
- The digit 4 is in the tens place. Its value is 4×10=40.
- The digit 7 is in the ones place. Its value is 7×1=7.
- The digit 5 is in the tenths place. Its value is $5 \times \frac{1}{10} = 0.5$.
- The digit 2 is in the hundredths place. Its value is $2 \times \frac{1}{100} = 0.02$.

- The digit 8 is in the thousandths place. Its value is $8 \times \frac{1}{1000} = 0.008$.

- The digit 4 is in the ten thousandths place. Its value is $4 \times \frac{1}{10,000} = 0.0004$.

- The digit 3 is in the hundred thousandths place. Its value is $3 \times \frac{1}{100,000} = 0.00003$.

When we add these values together, we find the value of the entire number:

$$2,000,000,000 + 700,000,000 + 30,000,000 + 5,000,000 + 900,000 + 80,000 + 7,000 + 600 + 40 + 7 + 0.5 + 0.02 + 0.008 + 0.0004 + 0.00003 = 2,735,987,647.52843$$

Place Value

Determine the place value of the underlined digit.

1. 6,325,386.2752 = _______________

2. 3,925,926.9409 = _______________

3. 535,606.83621 = _______________

4. 885,517.15639 = _______________

5. 39,508,212.059 = _______________

6. 1,786,616.4547 = _______________

7. 2,998,310.354 = _______________

8. 4,610,717,<u>3</u>20.1 = _______________________

9. 2,631,10<u>1</u>,778.5 = _______________________

10. 247,182.184<u>7</u>1 = _______________________

11. <u>4</u>5,301,189.76 = _______________________

12. 52,<u>9</u>71,638,000 = _______________________

13. 8,204,489.<u>6</u>297 = _______________________

14. 1,624,414.<u>1</u>937 = _______________________

15. 7,167,689.7<u>9</u>38 = _______________________

16. 8,531,341,579.4 = ________________________

17. 117,748.19927 = ________________________

18. 2,099,593,316.2 = ________________________

19. 6,895,883,843.2 = ________________________

20. 272,445,513.29 = ________________________

21. 5,085,130.9025 = ________________________

22. 114,174.60419 = ________________________

23. 472,721.20615 = ________________________

24. 9,536,005.873$\underline{4}$ = _______________________________

25. 1,370,81$\underline{5}$.0361 = _______________________________

26. 1,935,$\underline{3}$02.285 = _______________________________

27. 14$\underline{5}$,566.87509 = _______________________________

28. 8,127,132,42$\underline{0}$.9 = _______________________________

29. 65,767,449,71$\underline{1}$ = _______________________________

30. $\underline{9}$52,007,487.62 = _______________________________

31. 5,18$\underline{6}$,848.8389 = _______________________________

32. 6,5_0_4,456,709.8 = ______________________________

33. 7,847,5_1_5,613.6 = ______________________________

34. 97,523,_0_18.152 = ______________________________

35. 6_6_7,760,832.21 = ______________________________

36. 307,284.8900_7_ = ______________________________

37. 82,17_5_,117,755 = ______________________________

38. 420,622.9_3_166 = ______________________________

39. 7,918,_7_31.9217 = ______________________________

40. 209,946,060.5̲6̲ = _______________________________

41. 455,4̲55.78522 = _______________________________

42. 94,536,523.671̲ = _______________________________

43. 6̲44,073.29472 = _______________________________

44. 4̲8,331,155.725 = _______________________________

45. 3,02̲8,269,882.8 = _______________________________

46. 626,802.7905̲9̲ = _______________________________

47. 23,5̲01,976,744 = _______________________________

Adding Decimals

Adding decimals is like adding whole numbers, but we must align the decimal points carefully. For instance, when adding 49.88 and 45.78:

Step 1: Align the decimal points.

$$
\begin{array}{r}
49.88 \\
+\ 45.78 \\
\end{array}
$$

Step 2: Start adding from the rightmost digit (the ones place) and move to the left.

 Add 8 and 8: 8 + 8 = 16. Write down 6 in the ones place and carry over 1 to the tenths place.

$$
\begin{array}{r}
49.88 \\
+\ 45.78 \\
\hline
6 \\
\end{array}
$$

Step 3: Add the tenths place.

Add 1 (carried over from the previous step), 8, and 7: 1 + 8 + 7 = 16. Write down 6 in the tenths place and carry over 1 to the hundredths place.

$$
\begin{array}{r}
49.88 \\
+\ 45.78 \\
\hline
66 \\
\end{array}
$$

Step 4: Continue adding digits to the left until you reach the leftmost digit:

$$
\begin{array}{r}
49.88 \\
+\ 45.78 \\
\hline
9566 \\
\end{array}
$$

Step 5: Finally, write the sum with the decimal point directly below the decimal points in the original numbers.

$$
\begin{array}{r}
49.88 \\
+\ 45.78 \\
\hline
95.66 \\
\end{array}
$$

Subtracting Decimals

Subtracting decimals follows a process like adding decimals, except instead of adding the numbers, we subtract them.

Multiplying Decimals

Multiplying decimals is a lot like multiplying whole numbers, but we need to be careful about where we put the decimal point in the answer.

Step 1: Start by multiplying the numbers together, just like we do with whole numbers. Ignore the decimals for now.

Step 2: Count how many decimal places there are in the numbers we're multiplying. This will tell us how many decimal places our answer should have.

Step 3: Put the decimal point in the answer by starting from the right side of the number. Move the decimal point to the left as many places as there are in the total number of decimal places.

For example, let's multiply 4.5 by 2.5:

Step 1: Multiply the numbers as if they were whole numbers:

$$25 \times 45 = 1125.$$

Step 2: There is one decimal place in 2.5 and one in 4.5, making a total of two decimal places.

Step 3: Starting from the right side of the answer, count two places to the left and put the decimal point there.

So, the final answer is 11.25.

Remember to pay close attention to where the decimal point goes in the answer.

Dividing Decimals

Dividing decimals is a lot like dividing whole numbers, but we need to be careful about placement of decimal point in the answer.

Operations with Decimals

Complete the operations.

1.

$2.4 \overline{)8.2}$

2.

$$\begin{array}{r} 5.2 \\ \times\ 6.9 \\ \hline \end{array}$$

3.

$$\begin{array}{r} 64.93 \\ -\ 46.55 \\ \hline \end{array}$$

4.

$$\begin{array}{r} 7.0 \\ \times\ 6.6 \\ \hline \end{array}$$

5.

$8.2 \overline{)9.7}$

6.

$7.2 \overline{)4.1}$

7.

$$\begin{array}{r} 58.50 \\ +\ 80.46 \\ \hline \end{array}$$

8.

$$\begin{array}{r} 79.20 \\ -\ 40.58 \\ \hline \end{array}$$

9.

$$\begin{array}{r} 59.70 \\ +\ 51.91 \\ \hline \end{array}$$

10.

$$\begin{array}{r} 82.75 \\ -\ 68.11 \\ \hline \end{array}$$

11.

$3.5 \overline{)7.0}$

12.

$$\begin{array}{r} 71.01 \\ +\ 14.38 \\ \hline \end{array}$$

13.
$$4.6 \times 9.0$$

14.
$$2.1\overline{)1.1}$$

15.
$$79.32 + 51.58$$

16.
$$5.1\overline{)2.6}$$

17.
$$60.51 - 16.78$$

18.
$$7.0\overline{)3.8}$$

19.
$$91.74 - 80.44$$

20.
$$43.58 - 22.62$$

21.
$$90.75 + 12.29$$

22.
$$4.3\overline{)1.7}$$

23.
$$74.29 + 25.39$$

24.
$$39.25 - 20.83$$

25.
$$34.74 + 25.68$$

26.
$$3.1 \times 6.4$$

27.
$$24.64 - 13.47$$

28.
$$84.82 + 85.78$$

29.
$$8.7 \overline{)5.6}$$

30.
$$90.62 - 19.37$$

31.
$$1.0 \times 8.2$$

32.
$$96.49 - 51.20$$

33.
$$6.0 \overline{)2.4}$$

34.
$$98.86 - 93.53$$

35.
$$25.78 + 79.22$$

36.
$$8.3 \times 9.1$$

37.

$$76.36 + 92.85$$

38.

$$2.3 \times 2.1$$

39.

$$3.3\overline{)9.3}$$

40.

$$73.32 - 54.03$$

41.

$$80.43 - 45.68$$

42.

$$74.00 - 63.14$$

43.

$$43.06 + 67.65$$

44.

$$4.7\overline{)9.0}$$

45.

$$62.46 - 27.83$$

46.

$$8.8 \times 6.2$$

47.

$$9.4 \times 5.5$$

48.

$$3.6 \times 6.3$$

49.
$$1.4 \times 9.1$$

50.
$$7.5 \times 4.6$$

51.
$$34.44 - 12.82$$

52.
$$89.40 - 82.85$$

53.
$$88.71 + 79.25$$

54.
$$3.5\overline{)4.2}$$

55.
$$2.1\overline{)8.5}$$

56.
$$7.5 \times 9.9$$

57.
$$6.9\overline{)6.3}$$

58.
$$4.3\overline{)9.2}$$

59.
$$5.7 \times 9.6$$

60.
$$8.5\overline{)6.9}$$

61. $\begin{array}{r} 19.32 \\ +\ 59.37 \\ \hline \end{array}$	**62.** $\begin{array}{r} 7.8 \\ \times\ 8.8 \\ \hline \end{array}$	**63.** $\begin{array}{r} 99.32 \\ +\ 27.96 \\ \hline \end{array}$	**64.** $\begin{array}{r} 2.9 \\ \times\ 2.4 \\ \hline \end{array}$
65. $\begin{array}{r} 45.45 \\ +\ 26.55 \\ \hline \end{array}$	**66.** $\begin{array}{r} 21.36 \\ +\ 74.40 \\ \hline \end{array}$	**67.** $\begin{array}{r} 98.28 \\ +\ 93.14 \\ \hline \end{array}$	**68.** $\begin{array}{r} 52.00 \\ -\ 29.90 \\ \hline \end{array}$
69. $\begin{array}{r} 62.25 \\ +\ 11.36 \\ \hline \end{array}$	**70.** $\begin{array}{r} 9.8 \\ \times\ 7.9 \\ \hline \end{array}$	**71.** $\begin{array}{r} 5.0 \\ \times\ 1.3 \\ \hline \end{array}$	**72.** $8.0\overline{)7.9}$

<u>**Exponents**</u>

An exponent tells us how many times a number (called the base) is multiplied by itself. It is written as a superscript to the right of the base number. For example, in 2^3, 2 is the base and 3 is the exponent.

Rules:

1. **Product Rule**: When multiplying powers with the same base, add the exponents.

$$a^m \times a^n = a^{m+n}$$

For example:

$$2^3 = 2 \times 2 \times 2 = 8$$

$$3^2 \times 3^4 = 3^{2+4} = 3^6 = 3 \times 3 \times 3 \times 3 \times 3 \times 3 = 729$$

2. **Quotient Rule**: When dividing powers with the same base, subtract the exponents.

$$a^m \div a^n = a^{m-n}$$

For example:

$$5^3 \div 5^2 = 5^{3-2} = 5^1 = 5$$

3. **Power of a Power Rule**: When raising a power to another power, multiply the exponents.

$$(a^m)^n = a^{mn}$$

For example:

$$(2^2)^3 = 2^{2\times3} = 26 = 64$$

4. **Power of a Product Rule**: When raising a product to a power, distribute the power to each factor.

$$(ab)^n = a^n \times b^n$$

For example:

$$(2 \times 3)^2 = 2^2 \times 3^2 = 4 \times 9 = 36$$

5. **Power of a Quotient Rule**: When raising a quotient to a power, distribute the power to the numerator and denominator separately.

$$\left(\frac{a}{b}\right)^n = \frac{a^n}{b^n}$$

For example:

$$\left(\frac{4}{2}\right)^3 = \frac{4^3}{2^3} = \frac{64}{8} = 8$$

6. **Zero Exponent Rule**: Any nonzero number raised to the power of zero equals 11.

$$a^0 = 1$$

For example:

$$7^0 = 1$$

7. **Negative Exponent Rule**: A negative exponent means the reciprocal of the base raised to the positive exponent.

$$a^{-n} = \frac{1}{a^n}$$

For example:

$$2^{-3} = \frac{1}{2^3} = \frac{1}{8}$$

To evaluate expressions with exponents, we can use:

- **Repeated Multiplication**: Perform the multiplication indicated by the exponent.

- **Using the Rules of Exponents**: Apply the appropriate rule to simplify expressions involving exponents.

Square Roots

The square root of a number is a value that, when multiplied by itself, gives the original number. It's denoted by the symbol $\sqrt{}$.

For example, the square root of 9 is 3 because 3 * 3 = 9.

Cube Roots

The cube root of a number is a value that, when multiplied by itself twice, gives the original number. It's denoted by the symbol $\sqrt[3]{}$.

For example, the cube root of 8 is 2 because 2 * 2 * 2 = 8.

Exponents

Convert the values.

1. $5^3 =$ _______________

2. $13^4 =$ _______________

3. $4^4 =$ _______________

4. $17^4 =$ _______________

5. $16^4 =$ _______________

6. $12^3 =$ _______________

7. $7^3 =$ _______________

8. $20^{-2} =$ _______________

9. $18^2 =$ _______________

10. $4^3 =$ _______________

11. $19^{-2} =$

12. $2^{-2} =$

13. $9^4 =$

14. $8^2 =$

15. $18^{-2} =$

16. $16^{-2} =$

17. $2^2 =$

18. $10^3 =$

19. $17^{-3} =$

20. $14^{-3} =$

21. $11^3 =$

22. $5^4 =$

23. $17^2 =$ ___________

24. $20^4 =$ ___________

25. $20^{-3} =$ ___________

26. $10^{-2} =$ ___________

27. $9^{-3} =$ ___________

28. $9^3 =$ ___________

29. $16^2 =$ ___________

30. $6^2 =$ ___________

31. $9^2 =$ ___________

32. $19^{-3} =$ ___________

33. $11^{-3} =$ ___________

34. $12^{-2} =$ ___________

35. $3^{-2} =$ ______________

36. $17^{-2} =$ ______________

37. $20^{2} =$ ______________

38. $4^{-3} =$ ______________

39. $15^{-2} =$ ______________

40. $8^{-3} =$ ______________

41. $18^{3} =$ ______________

42. $13^{3} =$ ______________

43. $4^{-2} =$ ______________

44. $16^{-3} =$ ______________

45. $1^{3} =$ ______________

46. $19^{4} =$ ______________

47. $7^4 =$ ___________

48. $14^{-2} =$ ___________

49. $11^{-2} =$ ___________

50. $12^2 =$ ___________

51. $11^2 =$ ___________

52. $6^{-2} =$ ___________

53. $2^3 =$ ___________

54. $10^2 =$ ___________

55. $1^4 =$ ___________

56. $18^{-3} =$ ___________

Square and Cube Roots

Calculate the root of each value.

1. $\sqrt[4]{81}$ = _______________

2. $\sqrt{2,116}$ = _______________

3. $\sqrt[3]{1,000}$ = _______________

4. $\sqrt[3]{64}$ = _______________

5. $\sqrt[4]{16}$ = _______________

6. $\sqrt[3]{512}$ = _______________

7. $\sqrt[3]{729}$ = _______________

8. $\sqrt[4]{4,096}$ = _______________

9. $\sqrt{441}$ = _______________

10. $\sqrt{361}$ = _______________

11. $\sqrt[3]{8} =$ _______________

12. $\sqrt[4]{1} =$ _______________

13. $\sqrt{1,024} =$ _______________

14. $\sqrt[3]{125} =$ _______________

15. $\sqrt[3]{27} =$ _______________

16. $\sqrt{49} =$ _______________

17. $\sqrt[4]{6,561} =$ _______________

18. $\sqrt{81} =$ _______________

19. $\sqrt{64} =$ _______________

20. $\sqrt{9} =$ _______________

21. $\sqrt{576} =$ _______________

22. $\sqrt[3]{216} =$ _______________

23. $\sqrt[3]{1}$ = _______________

24. $\sqrt{1}$ = _______________

25. $\sqrt{625}$ = _______________

26. $\sqrt[3]{8{,}000}$ = _______________

27. $\sqrt{484}$ = _______________

28. $\sqrt[4]{1{,}296}$ = _______________

29. $\sqrt[4]{256}$ = _______________

30. $\sqrt{324}$ = _______________

31. $\sqrt{256}$ = _______________

32. $\sqrt{169}$ = _______________

33. $\sqrt{4}$ = _______________

34. $\sqrt[4]{10{,}000}$ = _______________

35. $\sqrt{100} =$ _______________

36. $\sqrt[4]{625} =$ _______________

37. $\sqrt[4]{2,401} =$ _______________

38. $\sqrt{16} =$ _______________

39. $\sqrt{225} =$ _______________

40. $\sqrt{3,721} =$ _______________

41. $\sqrt{144} =$ _______________

42. $\sqrt[3]{343} =$ _______________

43. $\sqrt{9,604} =$ _______________

44. $\sqrt[3]{1,728} =$ _______________

45. $\sqrt{784} =$ _______________

46. $\sqrt{2,500} =$ _______________

Percentage

Percentage is a way of expressing a number as a fraction of 100. It is commonly used to represent proportions, rates, and comparisons. The symbol "%" is used to denote percentages.

To calculate a percentage, we multiply the given number by the appropriate fraction or decimal equivalent.

How to calculate a percentage:

Convert Percentage to Decimal: If the percentage is given as a percentage value (e.g., 25%), convert it to its decimal equivalent by dividing by 100.

$$\text{For example, 25\% as a decimal is } \frac{25}{100} = 0.25$$

Multiply: Multiply the decimal equivalent of the percentage by the given number. This gives us the portion of the number that represents the percentage.

$$100 \times 0.25 = 25\%$$

Result: The result is the calculated percentage value.

For example, to calculate 25% of 80:

<u>Convert 25% to a decimal:</u> 25% = 0.25.

<u>Multiply 0.25 by 80:</u> $0.25 \times 80 = 20$. The result is 20.

Percent Word Problems

Percent word problems involve situations where percentages are used to calculate quantities or amounts. These problems often require converting percentages to decimals and then applying them to the given values.

For example:

Bella bought a pair of shoes for $90.00. If she paid an additional 90% for taxes, how much in total did she pay for the shoes?

- Bella bought a pair of shoes for $90.00.
- She paid an additional 90% for taxes.

Calculate 90% of $90:

Tax= 90% × 90

Tax= 0.90 × 90

Tax= $81

Add the tax amount to the original price:

Total cost= $90 + $81

Total cost= $171

Percentage

Find the percentage of given numbers.

1. 10% of ☐ = 60

2. 9% of 500 = ☐

3. 20% of ☐ = 60

4. ☐ of 900 = 720

5. ☐ of 300 = 45

6. 90% of 100 = ☐

7. ☐ of 40 = 0.4

8. 4% of 100 = ☐

9. 8% of ☐ = 16

10. 50% of 500 = ☐

11. ☐ of 400 = 24

12. ☐ of 10 = 20

13. ☐ of 40 = 40

14. 3% of 800 = ☐

15. 300% of ☐ = 2700

16. 75% of ☐ = 150

17. ☐ of 100 = 3

18. 2% of 900 = ☐

19. 5% of 50 = [ ]

20. [ ] of 800 = 80

21. [ ] of 300 = 270

22. 9% of 400 = [ ]

23. 8% of [ ] = 8

24. [ ] of 700 = 7

25. 40% of 100 = [ ]

26. 300% of [ ] = 2400

27. 15% of [ ] = 105

28. 7% of [ ] = 28

29. 80% of 200 = ☐

30. 35% of 10 = ☐

31. ☐ of 100 = 30

32. ☐ of 800 = 160

33. 4% of 300 = ☐

34. ☐ of 400 = 280

35. ☐ of 200 = 12

36. 200% of ☐ = 600

37. 25% of 500 = ☐

38. 60% of 200 = ☐

39. 100% of ☐ = 10

40. ☐ of 90 = 7.2

41. 60% of 500 = ☐

42. ☐ of 800 = 320

43. ☐ of 100 = 2

44. 25% of ☐ = 150

45. 20% of ☐ = 140

46. ☐ of 900 = 135

47. ☐ of 70 = 4.2

48. 75% of 600 = ☐

Convert: Ratio, Fraction, Percent, and Decimals

1.

	Ratio	Fraction	Percent	Decimal
a.		3/5		
b.			81.8%	
c.		13/20		
d.	8:12			
e.		1/3		
f.				0.625
g.	5:6			
h.				1
i.		3/13		
j.			25%	
k.				0.615
l.			55.6%	
m.				0.182
n.	4:16			
o.		7/9		

2.

	Ratio	Fraction	Percent	Decimal
a.		1/3		
b.				0.4
c.	1:4			
d.	5:9			
e.			66.7%	
f.	7:7			
g.	11:20			
h.	8:17			
i.			95%	
j.	17:18			
k.	4:8			
l.			50%	
m.			76.9%	
n.		2/3		
o.				0.917

3.

	Ratio	Fraction	Percent	Decimal
a.		2/4		
b.		1/1		
c.	3:14			
d.				0.091
e.				0.5
f.				0.6
g.		1/4		
h.	1:8			
i.	7:14			
j.			92.9%	
k.	4:6			
l.	16:20			
m.				0.571
n.		9/17		
o.	1:9			

ANSWERS

Page 1:   Operations with Integers

1. -2	**2.** -2	**3.** -6	**4.** 2	**5.** -9	**6.** 6	**7.** -6	**8.** 4	**9.** 5
10. -18	**11.** -11	**12.** 1	**13.** -21	**14.** -16	**15.** -23	**16.** -3	**17.** -14	**18.** -18
19. -20	**20.** 0	**21.** 4	**22.** 0	**23.** -11	**24.** 4	**25.** -7	**26.** -7	**27.** 10
28. -6	**29.** 1	**30.** 4	**31.** -11	**32.** -28	**33.** 15	**34.** 5	**35.** 4	**36.** -22
37. -14	**38.** 4	**39.** 7	**40.** 3	**41.** -7	**42.** 2	**43.** 14	**44.** 5	**45.** 14
46. 12	**47.** 7	**48.** 8	**49.** -6	**50.** 4	**51.** 7	**52.** -2	**53.** -20	**54.** -20
55. 8	**56.** 11	**57.** -12	**58.** 3	**59.** 6	**60.** 5	**61.** 5	**62.** -17	**63.** 8
64. -20	**65.** -11	**66.** 10	**67.** 4	**68.** 9				

Page 8:   Operations with Mixed Numbers

1. 10 2/3	**2.** 3 4/5	**3.** 86/153	**4.** 1 23/56	**5.** 1
6. 19/20	**7.** 1 7/30	**8.** 75 1/20	**9.** 5	**10.** 4 1/63
11. 3 4/9	**12.** 11 2/3	**13.** 11 7/15	**14.** 28 1/2	**15.** 6 3/28
16. 60 15/16	**17.** 7 8/35	**18.** 1 5/6	**19.** 36 1/9	**20.** 16 11/20
21. 28/31	**22.** 28/57	**23.** 60 1/14	**24.** 4 2/9	**25.** 9 1/4
26. 11 1/14	**27.** 1 43/72	**28.** 9/10	**29.** 1 7/297	**30.** 15 5/63
31. 11 1/2	**32.** 65/89	**33.** 16 3/8	**34.** 1 1/5	**35.** 8 23/70
36. 96/145	**37.** 1 37/224	**38.** 7	**39.** 52 2/15	**40.** 1 9/38
41. 1 81/224	**42.** 2	**43.** 63 8/9	**44.** 5 11/20	**45.** 1 27/28

Page 17:   Multiple Operations with Fractions

1. 1/12	**2.** 2 2/5	**3.** 3	**4.** 81/140
5. 6 1/4	**6.** 2 122/135	**7.** 1 11/40	**8.** 19/36
9. 47/378	**10.** 1 779/840	**11.** 97/216	**12.** 27/800
13. 1 26/35	**14.** 13/18	**15.** 143/360	**16.** 1 37/56
17. 11/27	**18.** 27/56	**19.** 1 23/90	**20.** 5 19/45
21. 7 7/90	**22.** 3 1/3	**23.** 85/216	**24.** 1 1/2
25. 45/256	**26.** 1 173/630	**27.** 1/42	**28.** 17/36
29. 7 1/9	**30.** 2 31/72	**31.** 41/120	**32.** 1 7/40
33. 1 11/150	**34.** 1 11/30	**35.** 1/10	**36.** 2 7/40
37. 149/180	**38.** 2747/3600	**39.** 97/168	**40.** 1 47/96

Page 27:   Place Value

1. 3 hundreds	**2.** 3 millions
3. 3 ten thousands	**4.** 5 hundredths
5. 5 hundred thousands	**6.** 4 tenths
7. 3 tenths	**8.** 3 hundreds
9. 1 thousand	**10.** 7 ten thousandths
11. 4 ten millions	**12.** 9 hundred millions
13. 6 tenths	**14.** 1 tenth
15. 9 hundredths	**16.** 3 hundred thousands
17. 4 tens	**18.** 2 billions
19. 8 ten thousands	**20.** 4 ten thousands

21. 5 ten thousandths

22. 0 hundredths

23. 2 tens

24. 4 ten thousandths

25. 5 ones

26. 3 hundreds

27. 5 thousands

28. 0 ones

29. 1 one

30. 9 hundred millions

31. 6 thousands

32. 0 ten millions

33. 1 ten thousand

34. 0 hundreds

35. 6 ten millions

36. 7 hundred thousandths

37. 5 millions

38. 3 hundredths

39. 7 hundreds

40. 5 tenths

41. 4 hundreds

42. 1 thousandth

43. 6 hundred thousands

44. 4 ten millions

45. 2 ten millions

46. 9 hundred thousandths

47. 5 hundred millions

Page 33: Operations with Decimals

1. 3.4	**2.** 35.88	**3.** 18.38	**4.** 46.20	**5.** 1.2	**6.** 0.6
7. 138.96	**8.** 38.62	**9.** 111.61	**10.** 14.64	**11.** 2	**12.** 85.39
13. 41.40	**14.** 0.5	**15.** 130.90	**16.** 0.5	**17.** 43.73	**18.** 0.5
19. 11.30	**20.** 20.96	**21.** 103.04	**22.** 0.4	**23.** 99.68	**24.** 18.42
25. 60.42	**26.** 19.84	**27.** 11.17	**28.** 170.60	**29.** 0.6	**30.** 71.25
31. 8.20	**32.** 45.29	**33.** 0.4	**34.** 5.33	**35.** 105.00	**36.** 75.53
37. 169.21	**38.** 4.83	**39.** 2.8	**40.** 19.29	**41.** 34.75	**42.** 10.86

43. 110.71	**44.** 1.9	**45.** 34.63	**46.** 54.56	**47.** 51.70	**48.** 22.68
49. 12.74	**50.** 34.50	**51.** 21.62	**52.** 6.55	**53.** 167.96	**54.** 1.2
55. 4.0	**56.** 74.25	**57.** 0.9	**58.** 2.1	**59.** 54.72	**60.** 0.8
61. 78.69	**62.** 68.64	**63.** 127.28	**64.** 6.96	**65.** 72.00	**66.** 95.76
67. 191.42	**68.** 22.10	**69.** 73.61	**70.** 77.42	**71.** 6.50	**72.** 1.0

Page 39: Exponents

1. 125	**2.** 28,561	**3.** 256	**4.** 83,521	**5.** 65,536
6. 1,728	**7.** 343	**8.** 1/400	**9.** 324	**10.** 64
11. 1/361	**12.** 1/4	**13.** 6,561	**14.** 64	**15.** 1/324
16. 1/256	**17.** 4	**18.** 1,000	**19.** 1/4913	**20.** 1/2744
21. 1,331	**22.** 625	**23.** 289	**24.** 160,000	**25.** 1/8000
26. 1/100	**27.** 1/729	**28.** 729	**29.** 256	**30.** 36
31. 81	**32.** 1/6859	**33.** 1/1331	**34.** 1/144	**35.** 1/9
36. 1/289	**37.** 400	**38.** 1/64	**39.** 1/225	**40.** 1/512
41. 5,832	**42.** 2,197	**43.** 1/16	**44.** 1/4096	**45.** 1
46. 130,321	**47.** 2,401	**48.** 1/196	**49.** 1/121	**50.** 144
51. 121	**52.** 1/36	**53.** 8	**54.** 100	**55.** 1

56. 1/5832

Page 44: Square and Cube Roots

1. 3	**2.** 46	**3.** 10	**4.** 4	**5.** 2	**6.** 8	**7.** 9	**8.** 8	**9.** 21
10. 19	**11.** 2	**12.** 1	**13.** 32	**14.** 5	**15.** 3	**16.** 7	**17.** 9	**18.** 9
19. 8	**20.** 3	**21.** 24	**22.** 6	**23.** 1	**24.** 1	**25.** 25	**26.** 20	**27.** 22

28. 6 **29.** 4 **30.** 18 **31.** 16 **32.** 13 **33.** 2 **34.** 10 **35.** 10 **36.** 5

37. 7 **38.** 4 **39.** 15 **40.** 61 **41.** 12 **42.** 7 **43.** 98 **44.** 12 **45.** 28

46. 50

Page 48: Percentage

1. 600 **2.** 45 **3.** 300 **4.** 80% **5.** 15% **6.** 90 **7.** 1%

8. 4 **9.** 200 **10.** 250 **11.** 6% **12.** 200% **13.** 100% **14.** 24

15. 900 **16.** 200 **17.** 3% **18.** 18 **19.** 2.5 **20.** 10% **21.** 90%

22. 36 **23.** 100 **24.** 1% **25.** 40 **26.** 800 **27.** 700 **28.** 400

29. 160 **30.** 3.5 **31.** 30% **32.** 20% **33.** 12 **34.** 70% **35.** 6%

36. 300 **37.** 125 **38.** 120 **39.** 10 **40.** 8% **41.** 300 **42.** 40%

43. 2% **44.** 600 **45.** 700 **46.** 15% **47.** 6% **48.** 450

Page 53: Convert: Ratio, Fraction, Percent, and Decimals

1.

	Ratio	Fraction	Percent	Decimal
a.	3:5	3/5	60%	0.6
b.	9:11	9/11	81.8%	0.818
c.	13:20	13/20	65%	0.65
d.	8:12	8/12	66.7%	0.667
e.	1:3	1/3	33.3%	0.333
f.	5:8	5/8	62.5%	0.625
g.	5:6	5/6	83.3%	0.833
h.	2:2	2/2	100%	1
i.	3:13	3/13	23.1%	0.231
j.	1:4	1/4	25%	0.25
k.	8:13	8/13	61.5%	0.615
l.	5:9	5/9	55.6%	0.556
m.	2:11	2/11	18.2%	0.182
n.	4:16	4/16	25%	0.25
o.	7:9	7/9	77.8%	0.778

2.

	Ratio	Fraction	Percent	Decimal
a.	1:3	1/3	33.3%	0.333
b.	4:10	4/10	40%	0.4
c.	1:4	1/4	25%	0.25
d.	5:9	5/9	55.6%	0.556
e.	6:9	6/9	66.7%	0.667
f.	7:7	7/7	100%	1
g.	11:20	11/20	55%	0.55
h.	8:17	8/17	47.1%	0.471
i.	19:20	19/20	95%	0.95
j.	17:18	17/18	94.4%	0.944
k.	4:8	4/8	50%	0.5
l.	1:2	1/2	50%	0.5
m.	10:13	10/13	76.9%	0.769
n.	2:3	2/3	66.7%	0.667
o.	11:12	11/12	91.7%	0.917

3.

	Ratio	Fraction	Percent	Decimal
a.	2:4	2/4	50%	0.5
b.	1:1	1/1	100%	1
c.	3:14	3/14	21.4%	0.214
d.	1:11	1/11	9.1%	0.091
e.	3:6	3/6	50%	0.5
f.	6:10	6/10	60%	0.6
g.	1:4	1/4	25%	0.25
h.	1:8	1/8	12.5%	0.125
i.	7:14	7/14	50%	0.5
j.	13:14	13/14	92.9%	0.929
k.	4:6	4/6	66.7%	0.667
l.	16:20	16/20	80%	0.8
m.	8:14	8/14	57.1%	0.571
n.	9:17	9/17	52.9%	0.529
o.	1:9	1/9	11.1%	0.111